I Am
Love

Live Life with Gratitude

Ashu Khanna

ISBN 979-8-89067-856-0

Other Titles by Ashu Khanna

I Am Freedom, Live Life with Awareness

I Am Abundance, Live a Life of Possibilities

I Am Perfection, Live Life Joyfully

Hare Krishna Hare Krishna
Krishna Krishna Hare Hare
Hare Rama Hare Rama
Rama Rama Hare Hare

To my parents who taught me
the power of love and faith

With Gratitude

This book is a dedication to my parents, who have been embodiments of selfless and unconditional love. I feel blessed to be born in a family where I have been nurtured with faith, love and courage and bestowed with the gift of knowledge to live life with Awareness.

My husband and children fill my life and embrace me in that circle of love. In my journey of search to inner contentment, I rediscovered the voice of Awareness. Mindfully, I have listened and traversed new grounds and peeled the layers, to live life with joy and love. Living with Awareness and staying tuned in to that voice, I share it as it arises. The theme and sequence of my books, *I Am Freedom, Live Life with Awareness; I Am Abundance, Live a Life of Possibilities; I Am Perfection, Live Life Joyfully* were revealed to me in moments of quietude. I bow to the benevolence of That Love, which is the cornerstone of our life. Filled with gratitude, my inner self has now expressed itself through poems. *I Am Love, Live Life with Gratitude* is an internal dialogue to the quest of centuries; What is life, Who Am I, How to live a life of purpose and joy. The poems reveal the path to living life with simplicity, beauty and happiness.

Awareness of our true self is a gift given to all human beings. Human life is designed to evolve to live in union with That inner love. We can choose to know it willingly or discover it gradually through force of circumstances. Every life is inter-connected to support this unfoldment. It is unknown to us when, how, who and through whom, we will rediscover our inner core. I marvel at the synchronicity of life and have observed people, events, circumstances occur in my life to support my evolution. My heartfelt gratitude to all the people who have touched my life and all the experiences that have helped me travel thus far.

We all have the power to awaken our inner voice and live life to the fullest moment to moment. I hope that the book inspires people to open their hearts to live in harmony with That Universal love, which like the rays of the sun is there for all, selfless and unconditional.

Contents

"Life is right here to love"

i seek

What is Life?

What is life?
How do I live life?
I am tired of fighting
I am tired of surviving

I only know fear
Fear of living
Fear of dying
Fear of being fearful

How do I know life?
When there is anger
Greed, jealousy and pain
And there is fear to let go

How do I drop the fear?
What do I hold onto?
Hold onto life
For life is to be lived

Life is a gift in itself
Live it with gratitude
For each moment is yours
To live with love and joy

Tides of Time

Life goes up
Life goes down
And with every tide
Life moves on

I try to hold onto the sails
Yet I rock before I know it
And then sometimes
I move gracefully along

I know I cannot avoid these tides
And some change the course of life
I can only learn to ride these tides
For they will always be a part of life

Time is the only healer
As I watch the play of life
And get stronger with each tide
And learn the rhythm of the tides

As I befriend the tides
And smile with each sway
Loving the ocean of life
Like a little child out to play

Fears

Where do you come from?
I didn't know you when I was born
I only knew love and trust
How did you enter my life?

Did I allow you entry unknowingly?
You were an unwelcome guest
Who made home for too long
And I did not even realize your overstay

I want to live again with love and trust
How do I tell you to go?
When I know you like my own
I am as attached to you as love

I know you are a guest, not the owner
I need to recognize that difference
Listen quietly to choose that love and trust
And the guest shall know its impermanence too

Life is a Journey

I started walking
Then I began running
Not knowing where am I going

I fell but I wanted to run
I hurt but I wanted to run
Not knowing where am I going

I was tired but I wanted to run
I was lost but I wanted to run
For I only knew how to run

I no longer know where I am going
I no longer know what I want
For I only know how to run

I left so many joys behind
I left so much love behind
For I was too busy running

When will I stop and enjoy
That joy, love and life
For which I started to run

Life is right here to love
It is for me to stop
Since it was only I who was running

"Hold onto the Love that spoilt me all along"

i want

Desires

We have likes
We have dislikes
We want life to be
As we like it to be

But do we know
What we truly want
For are we happy
When we get what we want

How do we solve this quest
How do we move forward
From this constant tussle
Of likes and dislikes

Can we change anything
Can we fight every moment
It is tiring to keep wanting so
Look around and see

Life as is in every moment
Enjoy it for what there is
Accept it for what it is
Live every moment as is

Jealousy

We look at others and think why
They look at me and also think why
We spend our life looking at another
And miss living our life as Me

What is it that makes us look at another
Are we not happy being Me
Do we want to swap our life with another
And take all that comes with the other

We want the best of others and me
Funny, do we even know what we want
We live as neither You nor Me
Oh, what a waste of a unique creation

Wake up, for there is only one Me
Else life will pass by quickly
Before you know the true Me
Let's make the most of living as Me!

Anger

Anger, who asked you to come
You are an uninvited guest
Stuck in my heart
I don't know how to let go
And invite love in my heart

I never listen
When I need to listen
I never speak
When I need to speak
So words come, as they want
When anger comes to me

Anger belongs only to you
For only you hold it in your heart
It is your burden alone
It does not belong to another
Let go, before it burns your heart
For only you can heal your heart

Listen carefully
For life is short
Speak carefully
For life is short
Laugh loudly
For life is short
Celebrate life
For life is short

Where is the place for anger
When there is so much to do
What is the need for anger
When there is a way to smile
Listen, laugh and celebrate
For life is short

Abundance

I am spoilt by my parents
I am spoilt by my family
I am spoilt by my friends
I am spoilt all along

I suffer because I am spoilt
I am angry because I am spoilt
I am lost because I am spoilt
I refuse to seek because I am spoilt

I don't know what to do
Because I am spoilt
How do I figure out what to do
When I am spoilt

Oh, how long will I stay stuck
And whine about life being such
Get up and seek freedom
Let go of all the wants

You have all you need
Just look around and see
There is so much love
Hold onto the love that spoilt me all along

"As being alive is an expression, of an emotion called Love!"

i insist

Tears

You come with joy
You come with sadness
You come with shame
You come with blame

When I am feeling sad
You release my sorrow
And make me feel lighter

When I am feeling frustrated
You release my anger
And make me see hope

When I am feeling happy
You express my joy
And make the world look brighter

Express freely and let them flow
Tears are after all an expression
Of being human!

Thoughts

Rivers flow joyously
Rivers cut through freely
Bouncing and dancing
Finding a new course

Thoughts flow
Endlessly and mindlessly
Do I know their course
Do I know their Source

How much do I know my thoughts
Yet, I allow my thoughts to block me
And stop from bouncing and dancing
And cutting a new course

Rivers know their destination
They know their source
What is the river without the Source
Another drop in the ocean

Thoughts forget their origination
Thoughts forget their destination
What is a thought without the Source
Another wave from the Source

Ego

I insist, you resist
You insist, I resist
We spend our life insisting and resisting
What stops us from accepting

What am I trying to achieve
By playing this game of wining and losing
I only lose love and I only gain pain
Yet, I insist on playing this game

Time and again I lose
Never failing to stop and ask
What's the purpose of it all
When I get nothing at all

Stop, oh foolish one and think
Why did I make you play this game
To chisel away that veil and look within
To know the love that sits within

Emotions

Thank you for being a part of me
I feel life, I live life, I taste life
For emotions are given to me

Why run away from being emotional
Why cringe at the thought of emotions
For emotions were given to me

I experience each emotion
I experience life at every level
For emotions were given to me

Sometimes I laugh, sometimes I cry
And observe each emotion
As I let them pass through me

I am aware of my emotions
I vulnerably share my emotions
For I am a human here to live

I feel alive at every moment
As being alive is an expression
Of an emotion called Love!

"And smile at my humanness each time"

i reflect

Silence

Silence so profound
Yet so loud
I hear you tell me
Truth of life

In that quiet voice
That only I can hear
In my heart
What is right for me

How do I do
What you ask me to do
Even when I know
It is right for me

Make me silent inside
To do what I need to do
Give me courage inside
To do what is right for me

Oh, it is for you to be silent
And listen to me speak
For I am always with you
To help you do what is right for you

Witness

Flowers have
All the fragrances that can be
Birds have
All the colours that can be
Animals have
All the sounds that can be
You & I have
All the beauty that can be

Then what is missing?
The nose
Forgets to smell
The eyes
Forget to see
The ears
Forget to hear
You & I
Are too busy to be

How can
You & I remember to be
I don't know
It is for You & I
To want to listen
To the sounds of laughter
And enjoy the splendour
And just be!

Inner Voice

Who are you
Where do you come from
Where do you go
How do you come

I spent years trying to know
Only to realise
I don't need to know everything
I only need to feel you

You are my guide
Like none other
You are mine
Like none other

You are in everyone
You know everything
You are always there
I only need to feel you

You are my strength
You are my happiness
For you fill me with love
Like none other

Forgiveness

I did what I thought was right
Doing my best each time
Yet, I didn't always get what I wanted

I ask myself
Can I always get what I want
Can I always know what is right

After all, every act is done for the best
And for first time at that moment in time
Then how can I always be right

Guilt and regret are emotions in hindsight
I can only try not to fall next time
And be gentle and forgive

I can try to stay present to each moment
For life is unknown to me
And smile at my humanness each time

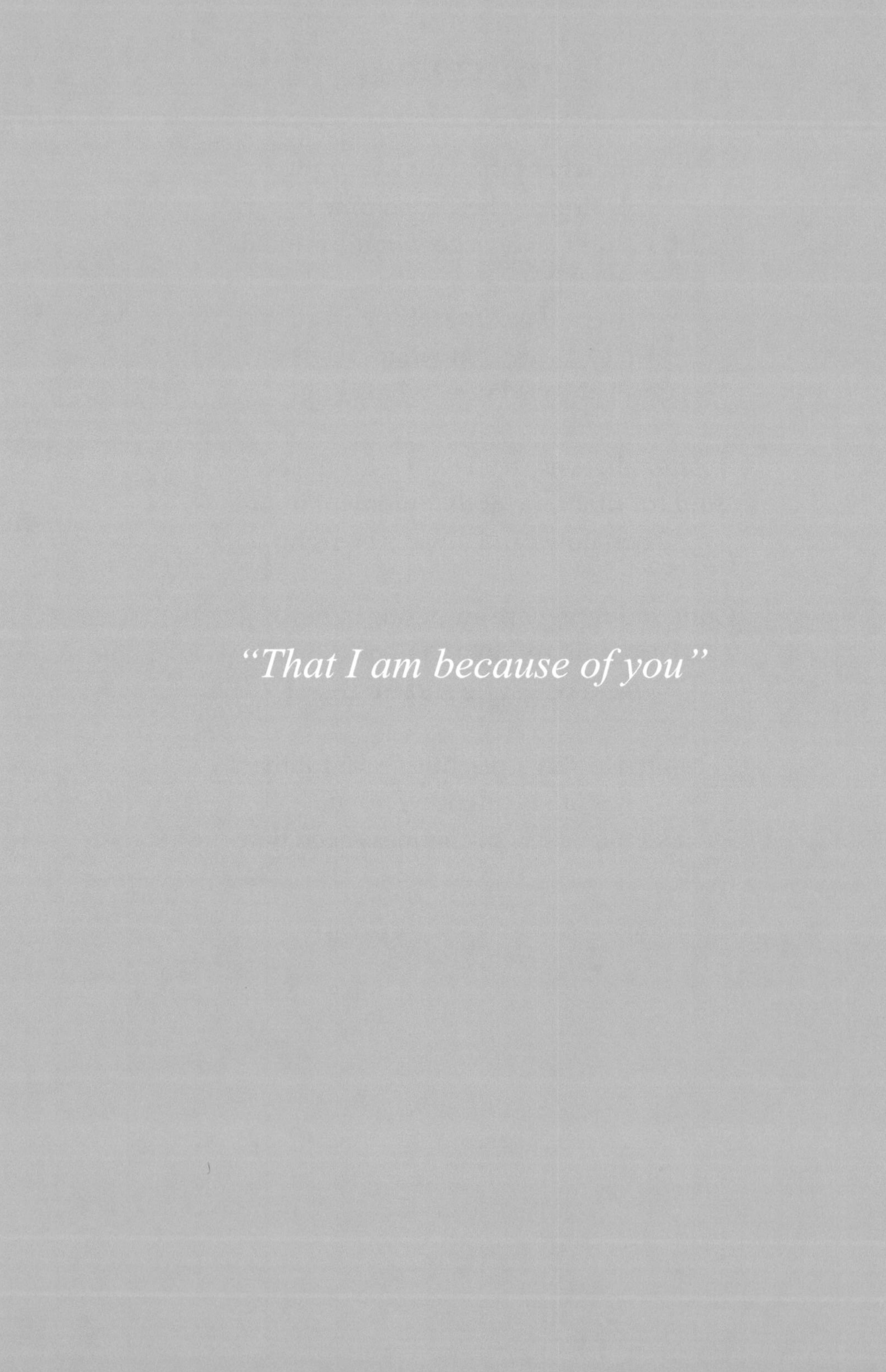
"That I am because of you"

i thank

Relationships

What is a relationship
Is it a connect of two minds
Is it a connect of two souls

Where I accept you
And you accept me
For each as we are

Only that is the truth
For love focuses only
On both being right

Where I give some
And you give some
For only the relationship matters

There is no greater truth
Because nothing else matters
As only the relationship matters

Childhood

Laughter, play, fun and games
Friends and family filled with love
Every morning is bright and shining
What a joy to be a child

The days of childhood flew by
Filling life with memories to cherish
Making me smile even today
Every time I reminisce on those days

Where did that child get lost
I forgot to keep that wondrous child alive
I got too stuck in being a certain way
And made life the way it is today

Remembering that child
I travelled back in time
To recreate that joy and contentment
That was all a part of me

I enjoy that child today
As I laugh and play
Loving every moment of life
Knowing that life is just a game

Family

Brought up with love and care
With every ounce of sacrifice
To make my future bright
Family held me up always like divine love

I expect them to understand always
Without saying a word for they are family
I forget they are as human as me
In need of love and assurance

I take more from family
I give more to friends
I expect more from family
I expect none from friends

What a paradox to live with
Then I complain there is no love
Then I cry that no one understands
Who should I blame but myself

For family are the friends gifted to me
That I take for granted for it is free
Like the divine love that comes with birth
Holding me up forever free

Breath

Who are you
You've been with me forever
Serving me selflessly
And silently being with me

I even forget you exist
Till I see you leave another
Then I grieve for a moment
And once again forget your existence

How long will it take me to know
That I am because of you
You are my best friend
Yet I forget your existence

When will I learn, it's time to befriend
For you are the only one who knows me
As you have travelled with me forever
And will always serve me as none other

"That which sees as is, is Love"

i realise

Perfection

I hear that I am beautiful
I hear that I am not the best
I get happy; I get sad
What do I believe?

I want to be beautiful
I want to be perfect
I try to look good
I strive for perfection

What should I do?
I wonder what is perfection
I look around and what do I see
Everything and everyone is unique

Now I wonder what is unique about me
I peep inside and what do I discover
That I am perfect and unique as I am
For I am born to be Me!

Living as Me is the best tribute
To that which created me
And play my role to perfection
For I am born to be Me!

Gratitude

I am blessed for what I have
What more can I want or need
Yet I am foolish not to see

I keep looking and wanting
Not knowing that there is nothing missing
Because I am foolish not to know

Even when I see what I have
I find it difficult to shed my beliefs
As I foolishly resist to accept

I question, why; I hear, why not,
For you get, what you deserve
I can't keep living foolishly rejecting That Love

Have gratitude for That which has given
Stop being foolish and embrace That Love
Take charge and do what is right with That Love

Humility

Sometimes I am wrong
Sometimes I am right
Sometimes I know
Sometimes I don't

I know I cannot stop falling
I know I cannot stop climbing
As I will walk on new roads
For I am born to seek

I accept my path
Knowing its mine to walk
For we all have one
Knowingly or not

As I walk along
I can cry and weep
Or I can laugh and play
Knowingly or not

As I joyously embrace my path
And respect the might of Nature
I live everyday as is
Being who I am

Love is...

How do I understand you
I have been in love
I have received love
I have lost love

Yet I didn't know what is love
It has made me blossom
It has made me cry
It has made me smile

I still didn't know what is love
Then I asked
How would I want love to be
That which sees 'as is', is Love

"For Nature fulfills the very wish of change"

i explore

What do I Know?

What do I see
What do I hear
What do I know
Nothing
I see what I want to see
I hear what I want to hear
I know what I think I know
Nothing

I live knowing nothing
Yet I think I know
Everything
How limited am I
I don't know
Because I know what I know

I open my heart to listen
I open my eyes to observe
Suddenly what do I know
That I knew nothing

That is the best place to be
Knowing nothing
And discovering everything
Miracles, Joy and Love

Curiosity

Life changes moment to moment
Did my thinking change with each moment
Oh no, I kept thinking the same way
For I didn't see the changes

I was so sure of my thinking
That I did not need to change
What a joke, to think so
That I knew more than life

Alas, tired of being stuck
I asked myself why and how
That moment changed my life
For finally I had the courage to ask

I failed, I felt rejected, I felt pain
I succeeded, I felt accepted, I felt joy
Again, I asked why and how
And I tried again and again

Till I realised that curiosity is the only way
To knowing how to live life
For there will be no answers
And there will always be change

Explore

How do I walk this path of life?
How do I not fall?
How do I stay on top?

Now, let me ask myself
Have I always stayed on top?
Have I never fallen?

Why put this pressure on me
When I know I enjoy trying
I want newness; I want freshness

It is time I accepted
The changes that I invite
From childhood to adulthood

Just be an explorer of this journey of life
Cherishing experiences with gratitude
For Nature fulfills the very wish of Change!

Life is a Mystery

I am living this life for the first time
I want to know will I fail or succeed
I want to know will I be happy or sad
I want all the answers now

Then I say life is a bore
I don't want surprises or mysteries
Then I say life is a chore
I want all the answers now

Do I want to be a scientist
Do I want to be an explorer
Inventing or discovering by the days
Or do I want all the answers now

Life is full of mysteries
Life is full of surprises
Make life as you want it to be
Why want all the answers now

Enjoy the mystery
Enjoy the surprises
Life is perfect in every moment
For that moment is an answer itself

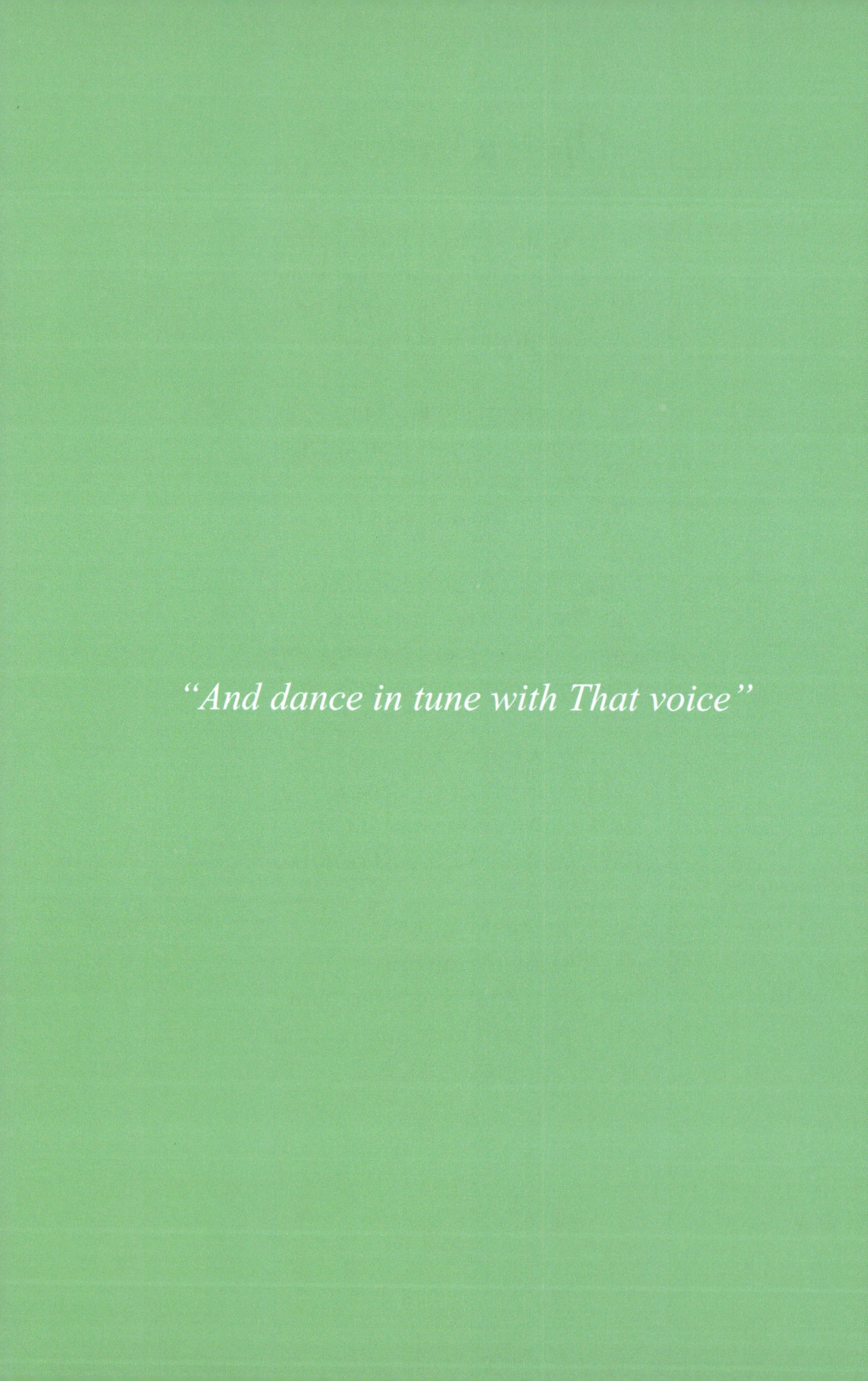
"And dance in tune with That voice"

i trust

Patience

There is so much noise all around
I can barely hear myself speak
I can barely hear another speak
Does anyone care to listen at all

I go silent just to observe all around
And I become aware of the noise within
There are thoughts clashing all the time
Oh, it's even more noisy than outside

What should I do to quieten
What should I do to listen
As I observe and absorb
Oh, what do I discover

I need to be patient
And listen to what's within
To quietly move around
And silently flow with it all

Choice

Do I have a choice
Do I not have any
Who am I

Just another creation
Living an illusion
And making it so real

Foolishly caught
In that illusion
By making it so real

The script is written
Though not known
Be wise to follow

For it is the only choice
Live it well
For I have that Choice

Surrender

I accept your might
Knowing your role in life
Feeling gratitude
For That abundance

I flow with you
Expressing my love for you
Because I owe you
For That love

That love is my strength
That love is my faith
That love is my breath
That love holds me

I surrender to That Love
That flows through me
For I am just an instrument
Of That Love

Happiness

I run after you
I run for you
And then I run away from you

How can I find you
I am confused
And feeling foolish
After running everywhere

I sit back feeling desperate
Not knowing what to do
Once again I ask myself
Where can I find you

Stop running
Seek and listen quietly
Happiness is where it belongs
Always in me

As I listen to that voice
And dance in tune with that voice
And be as I am meant to be
I feel that happiness in me

"Sharing the love in my heart"

i act

Dreams

I am a dreamer who dreams big
For what does it cost to dream
Who can question or doubt my dreams
For they are mine to see or be

And then I question my own dreams
Are they too large to be?
When I see some come true or not
And some fall away or change

I wonder what is it that I could do
To make my dreams come true
Who can question my dreams but me
Who can make them happen but me

I need to stay true to my dreams
For they are meant for me
And walk the path step by step
Always believing in the dream

Hope

I hope I get what I want
I hope that tomorrow will be

Our hope keeps us alive
And our hope keeps us from living

Are we stuck in wishful thinking
Or are we living with faith

How do I know it's one or the other
Only awareness can tell me the difference

When I live with awareness, I know
I will be ok because I Am That

Purpose of Life

You touch my heart
You touch my soul
You surround my thoughts
You make me want to be

What should I do
How should I do
I think, I worry
There is little that I know

My heart pushes me forward
As I follow this bright road
I ask my heart
Where will you take me

Keep walking trustingly
Holding the hand of Truth
For it is the only choice
That your heart knows

Live Creatively

There is so much beauty
Different colours and shapes
I really wonder and ask
How did so much come to be

Like a canvas painted afresh
Every morning a kaleidoscope
Inspired by this miracle
I feel excited to learn anew

As I go quiet and curious
Words just bubble out
Writing pages I never knew
As I let them flow and flow

Creating my own canvas
Loving the beauty of life
For words is my way
Of sharing the love in my heart

"An instrument of love"

i lead

Love Yourself

It matters when people say no
It matters when people judge
It matters when people assume
It matters when people expect

How long will you be silent
How long will you be angry
How long will you be unhappy
You have to stand up for yourself

You get what you deserve
Not what you want
Life is totally fair
You have the power to choose

To matter to yourself
Not take yourself for granted
To love yourself for who you are
Always remember this truth

Home

A place called home
Warm and abundant
Who lives there

King of joy
Queen of hearts
Princes of laughter

Fragrance of food
Rustle of breeze
Green leaves, pink flowers

Who made this home
Family, the circle of love
To hug and hold

Own your Power

I stand tall
I stand high
I stand straight

When I align within
And not succumb
To my emotions

For I have the power
To conquer all
With the strength within

And be who I am
An instrument of love
Born to serve & love

Standing Tall

Standing tall
Loved by all
Embracing one and all

The energy of love
Flows through me
Uninterrupted

Awakening and healing
Their hearts
To flow with love

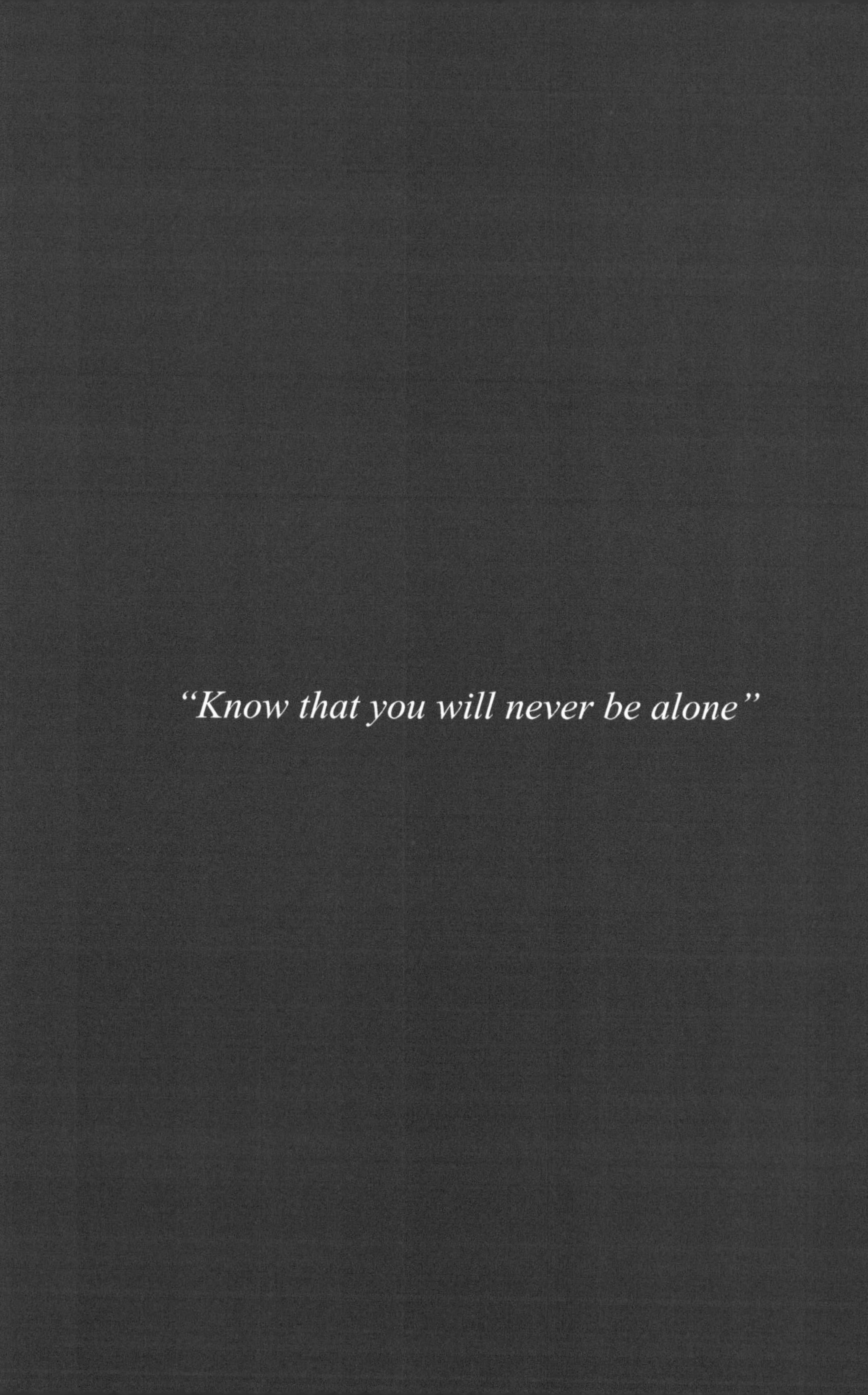
"Know that you will never be alone"

i grow

Change

How do I live life
How do I not fall
How do I stay on top

Now let me ask myself
Do I enjoy being the same
Do I enjoy doing the same

I want newness
I want freshness
For I invite the changes

Then what I can do best
Is to accept the gift of change
And be strong to ride the waves

Enjoy the journey of life
Cherish every experience with gratitude
For nature fulfils the very wish of change

Circle of life

Wide expanse covered with grass
Small shrubs and tall trees
Water holes scattered along

Lions, deer, giraffes, elephants
All existing together in this expanse
As that's the circle of life

Sometimes ferocious, sometimes meek
Youth and old age, spare none
Neither you, nor me

Wake up, before life catches up
Stay youthful and cherish this life
Life is just a merry-go-round

Imagination

Fluffy clouds like soft cotton wool
Floating above cradled in a bubble
I looked around in wondrous awe

Blue sky with light shining bright
The horizon afar and yet near
Opening the doors to imagination

My heart stopped beating
My eyes wide as I looked
At this miraculous sight

A picture created by the artist
Who keeps changing the vistas
For you and me to play and smile

Keep Climbing

I sat in quietude in the mountains
Listening to the voice of the heart

The voice said,
Keep climbing, let go of all fear
Trust your destiny and just walk

Know that you will never be alone
For I will always be holding your hand

Just surrender to the power of my love
Life will become playful like the breeze

"Living true to myself is happiness"

i know

Life is Simple

Life was simple
Till I made it complex
And then everything was difficult
So I could no longer get it

The sun rises and sets everyday
The earth moves around the sun
Yet I could not see
There is a law to everything

I knew I had to understand life
For I could not go on just as is
I looked silently at life all around
And I saw that there is a law

I had to know this law
To make life simple again
For that's what it was to be
Happy, blissful and easy to be

Life is Beautiful

How often do I simply look?
Having no thoughts
Soaking up with my heart
Enjoying what's there

As I sit quietly looking around
I see wonders of the world
Colours, shapes and forms
Endless and beyond

I am awe struck by the beauty of all
I miss what's right here
For I am busy doing wonder what
Then I ask what's life all about

There is so much I don't know
Life has given me a chance to know
To love and enjoy the beauty of all
For Life is right here and now

I can live and cherish this life
Or squander it like a fool
For once I know that life is right here
It is for me to live that Truth

Life is a Play

Nature nurtures me with love
Nature nurtures me with challenge
Nature gives me everything I need
Yet I don't recognise its love and play

I am so lost in my clutter
I miss that play altogether
Life happens around me at all times
Yet I can't grasp its love and play

How do I see and enjoy life as a play
Rather than become the main actor
How do I keep pace with change
When I feel fear in its vastness

Think deep and listen to your paradox
You are just one of the actors
You know you will be challenged
You know you will be loved

Let go and play your part
For life is just a play of That Love
There are many there to love and play
The screen will change, so will the play

Live with Awareness

People come, people go
Events come, events go
The scene keeps changing
How aware am I of this change

Do I know that I too change
Sometimes happy, sometimes not
Oh, I wish I could always be happy
Than live like a bumbling fool

How aware am I of myself
To know how to be happy
How aware am I of others
To know how to be happy

Happiness is always with me
It is for me to choose to be
Living true to myself is happiness
For then there is nothing more to be

"I am nothing without That Love..."

i am

I Am...

I wonder who I am
I want to be happy
I want to be loved
I want to be successful

Am I truly what you see
Even I don't know Who Am I
Who will tell me
Who but I can help know me

Did I always know me
Where did I get lost
I searched everywhere, not knowing
I was always there with me

Hidden deep beneath
The layers of illusion
I had only to peep
Deep within to know That

I am as happy as I choose to be
I am as loving as I choose to be
I am as silent as I choose to be
I am...

Life Is...

Life occurs now
Yet we don't see how
We resist; we insist
And we refuse to accept

What fools are we
To think we can change
That exists as is
For that's how life is

We struggle; we bungle
We make life hard
Not wanting to embrace
For life as is

If only we could
Life would be a smile
And every moment a joy
For life is...

That Is...

I know there is love all around
Yet I believe that I exist without
I live life in that arrogance
Never pausing to say thank you

Because I believe I exist without
How foolish am I to think so
How foolish am I to want my love to be known
When that too rests on That Love

What is my identity without That Love
I am nothing without That Love
Just a foolish voice making noise
For there is no expression without That Love

"Gently with the wind"

i flow

Prayer

I pray for courage and love
I pray to know what to do
I follow the voice
Knowing that as my Truth

As I walk slowly
I take a pause
To listen to That Love
That lives inside me

It takes strength to grow
It takes strength to walk slow
It takes strength to be
Pray, for it is the only way

That Love is there for me
That Love is there for you
For I am just another child
Born special to be

Faith

Am I weak
Am I strong
Am I brave
Am I not

How do I know
Till I try and push
There is no boundary
Except my own

The walls can fall
If I choose to break free
For when I look back
I know I can

I have to step out
And take that leap
To discover my Truth
For it is mine to know

Grace

I am blessed
I am grateful
I bow in reverence
To That love

For who am I to know
Why Me or Why not Me
I listen deeply
To That voice

It guides me
Slowly and surely
For who am I to know
What is best for me?

Knowing it is with me
Is enough for me
For it is my true friend
Always there for me

Flow with Life

Born gentle and kind
The world thought me to be mild
Little did I know my strength
For I was always called mild

Wanting to be strong
I fought forever
Only to discover
Strength was hidden within

I had to walk this path
For I had to discover
To spread gentle love
I need to be strong

It takes strength to give
It takes strength to take
And it takes strength to flow
Gently with the wind

"For every moment is ours to choose anew"

i choose

Live Free

Clouds are
Not a part of the sky or the earth
Yet they belong
They know no fear
Because they know their part
They float along
They play along
They are powerful
Yet they are light
They are free

I am free
My family is my earth
That love is my sky
I flow in between
Doing my own thing
Knowing I am never alone
I cry, I smile, I play, I hide
That's all a part of me
Because I know I belong

Live Relevantly

Do I want to be successful
Do I want to be significant
Do I want to be relevant
Oh, what do I want to be

Do I matter to the world
Does the world matter to me
If the world doesn't matter to me
Why will I matter to the world

Think, what do you want
Success depends on another
Significance too depends on another
Relevance is yours to be

For it is only when you care
Are you relevant to another
Success and significance no longer matter
For it is about how you wish to be

Live with Mastery

Tired and frustrated, I look up
And I ask, Why Me
A voice replies, Why not you

What have I done to deserve
Ha, says the voice within
You get what you choose

For its all upto you
Why Me or Why not Me
You can listen to that voice or not

You can be your own master
Choose how you wish to live
And life will come back as is

Live Joyfully

What's so unique about today
That makes us promise to live another way
What stops us from living so everyday
When everyday is a new day

It's for you and me to decide to live
Making everyday a fresh start
And live life as we want
And fulfill dreams of our heart

The biggest gift we have
Is the gift of free will
Choose wisely how to live
For this moment is yours

Every morning offers a chance to begin anew
Every sunset offers a chance to close doors
Every moment offers a chance to smile
For every moment is ours to choose anew